A TASTING PARTY

by Jane Belk Moncure
illustrated by Lois Axeman
created by The Child's World

CP CHILDRENS PRESS, CHICAGO

Cover and Title Page
Designed by Dolores Hollister

Library of Congress Cataloging in Publication Data

Moncure, Jane Belk.
  A tasting party.

  (The Five senses)
  Summary: Flowers, leaves, seeds, roots,
fruits, dairy foods, and meats are sampled
at different types of food tasting parties.
    1. Taste—Juvenile literature. (1. Taste)
I. Axeman, Lois ill. II. Title. III. Series:
Moncure, Jane Belk.   Five senses.
QP456.M66   152.1'67   82-4411
ISBN 0-516-03253-4   AACR2

A TASTING PARTY

There are many
kinds of parties—
like birthday parties,

Halloween parties,

Valentine parties,
and even pajama parties.

Have you ever been to a tasting party,
a food-tasting party?
Wake up your taste buds, and come along.

What do you taste with?
Your tongue, of course.
At a food-tasting party,
you can taste many kinds of food.

Some foods taste

sweet—

like raisins and cherries

and ripe strawberries.

Other foods taste
salty—

like ham and
bacon,

popcorn
and
potato chips.

Some foods taste

sour—

like pickles

and lemons.

Others taste

bitter—

like little green apples

and not-quite-ripe grapes.

There are different kinds of tasting parties
where you can taste different treats.

Come to a

flower-tasting party.

Wake up your taste buds and come along.

These flowers are not the marigolds and daisies in your garden. These flowers are

cauliflowers
and broccoli buds.

Vitamins A and C say:

Flowers have lots of "Go Power!"

Pass the flowers, please.

How do these flowers taste?

The leaves on a tree
are crisp and green.
Leaves on trees are for giraffes,
but people do eat leaves.
Come to our

leaf-tasting party.

Use your tongue
to taste

cabbage,

spinach,

mint,

parsley.

How do these leaves taste?

Do you feed the animals seeds in winter?
Many people do.
Birds, squirrels, and chipmunks
all like seeds.
People eat seeds too.

Come to a
seed-tasting party.

Use your tongue to taste tiny seeds—

sesame,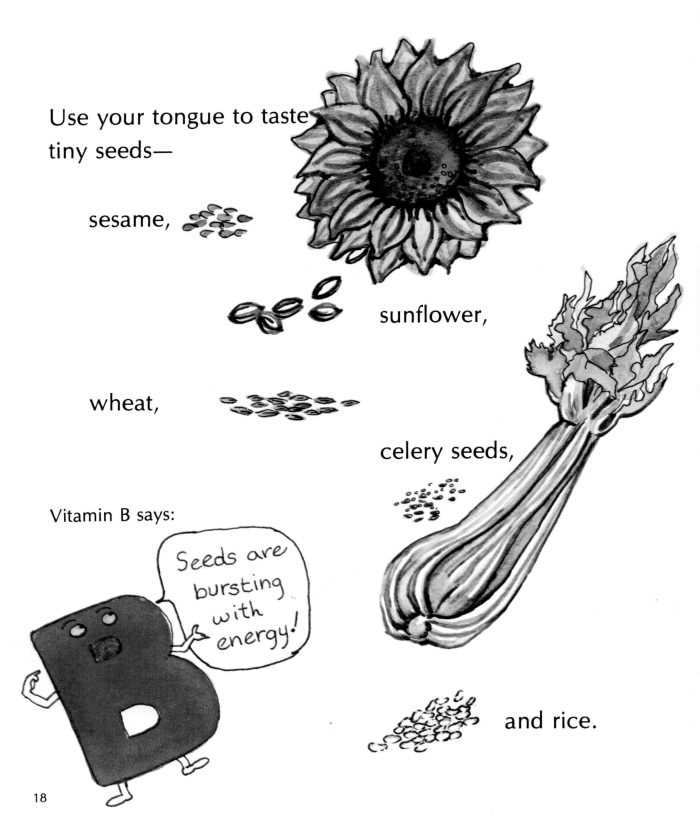

sunflower,

wheat,

celery seeds,

Vitamin B says:

Seeds are bursting with energy!

and rice.

Taste middle-sized seeds—
peanuts,

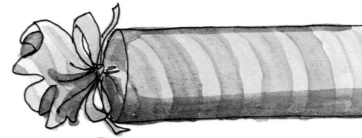

green peas,

lima beans,

oats,

pumpkin,

squash,

and popcorn.

Taste a giant seed,
the biggest seed
in all the world—
a coconut seed.

How do these seeds taste?

In spring, we plant seeds.
Soon roots grow down below the ground.
Bunnies like roots.
You may like them too.
So come to our

root-tasting party.

Use your tongue to taste a

parsnip,   beet,   radish,   turnip.

How do they taste?

Vitamins A and C say:

Give a hoot! Taste a root!

Pass the roots, please.

In summer, fruit grows on trees and vines,
on bushes and tiny plants.
Come to a
fruit-basket party.

Use your tongue
to taste a
banana,

pineapple,

orange, tomato, and some cherries.
How do fruits taste?

23

Flower parties, leaf parties, root parties, seed parties, and fruit parties.
Are there any other tasting parties?
Of course!

How about a

dairy-food-tasting party?

Join us at the farm.

milk,

and ice cream.

How do dairy foods taste?

We will have one more party.
This one's a
picnic-party.
Are you ready?
Come along.

Use your tongue to taste meats—

beef,   pork,   turkey,

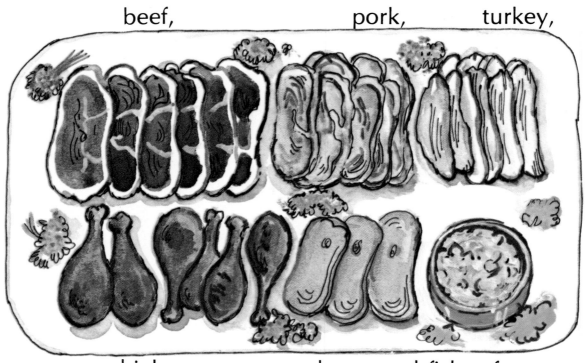

chicken,   ham, and fish, of course.

Taste other
protein foods too—

eggs,

beans,

Vitamin B says:

These foods
make you strong.

and nuts.

How do these foods taste?

How many foods have you tasted?
How many more foods can you taste?
From now on, remember . . .
meals and snacks make
great food-tasting parties!